MAP AND TRACK BIOMES & ANIMALS

MAP AND TRACK GRASSLANDS

NANCY DICKMANN

Crabtree Publishing Company
www.crabtreebooks.com

CRABTREE
PUBLISHING COMPANY
WWW.CRABTREEBOOKS.COM

Author: Nancy Dickmann

Editors: Sarah Eason, Honor Head, Reagan Miller

Proofreaders and indexers: Tracey Kelly, Wendy Scavuzzo

Editorial director: Kathy Middleton

Design: Jessica Moon

Cover design: Katherine Berti

Photo research: Jean Coppendale

Prepress and print coordination: Katherine Berti

Written, developed, and produced by Calcium

Every attempt was made to verify the accuracy of the maps from multiple sources. Sources may differ.

Photo Credits:

b=Bottom, l=Left, r=Right, m=Middle, t=Top

Inside: Shutterstock: p. 14; aaabbbccc: p.11; 28t; Andaman: p. 18b; Agnieszka Bacal: p. 10; Tomas Calle Boyero: p. 12; Katarina Christenson: p. 26; Lucian Coman: p. 24; Curioso: p.20; EcoPrint: p. 27; Four Oaks: p. 18t; Paula French: p. 21; Kerry Hargrove: p. 9t; Jukka Janunen: p. 9b; DePlanque Joel: p. 16; Karamysh: p. 15t; Jess Kraft: pp. 1c, 11; Dagmara Ksandrova: p. 17t; kyslynskahal: p. 22; ThomasLenne: pp. 3, 29; Wang LiQiang: p. 5b; Stuart G Porter: p. 23t; Anatoily Lukich: p. 23b; NaturesMomentsuk: pp. 1r, 8b; Nektarstock: p. 17b; Michael Potter11: p. 25; Ondrej Prosicky: 19; Ron Ramtang: p. 7; Studiolaska: p. 8t; TTphoto: p. 5t; Txanbelin: p. 4; Victor Tyakht: p. 13; Cathy Withers-Clarke: p. 28b; HelloRH Zcool: p. 15b.

Maps: Jessica Moon, Katherine Berti

Cover: Shutterstock

Library and Archives Canada Cataloguing in Publication

Dickmann, Nancy, author
Map and track grasslands / Nancy Dickmann.

(Map and track biomes and animals)
Includes index.
Issued in print and electronic formats.
ISBN 978-0-7787-5367-4 (hardcover).--
ISBN 978-0-7787-5379-7 (softcover).--
ISBN 978-1-4271-2201-8 (HTML)

1. Grassland ecology--Juvenile literature. 2. Grassland animals--Juvenile literature. 3. Grasslands--Maps--Juvenile literature. 4. Cartography--Juvenile literature. I. Title.

QH541.5.P7D53 2019 j577.4 C2018-905628-2
C2018-905629-0

Library of Congress Cataloging-in-Publication Data

Names: Dickmann, Nancy, author.
Title: Map and track grasslands / Nancy Dickmann.
Description: New York : Crabtree Publishing Company, 2019. | Series: Map and track biomes and animals | Includes index.
Identifiers: LCCN 2018049859 (print) | LCCN 2018056557 (ebook) | ISBN 9781427122018 (Electronic) | ISBN 9780778753674 (hardcover) | ISBN 9780778753797 (pbk.)
Subjects: LCSH: Grasslands--Juvenile literature. | Grassland ecology--Juvenile literature.
Classification: LCC GB571 (ebook) | LCC GB571 .D53 2019 (print) | DDC 551.45/3--dc23
LC record available at https://lccn.loc.gov/2018049859

Crabtree Publishing Company
www.crabtreebooks.com 1-800-387-7650

Printed in the U.S.A./032019/CG20190118

Published in Canada
Crabtree Publishing
616 Welland Ave.
St. Catharines, Ontario
L2M 5V6

Published in the United States
Crabtree Publishing
PMB 59051
350 Fifth Avenue, 59th Floor
New York, New York 10118

Published in the United Kingdom
Crabtree Publishing
Maritime House
Basin Road North, Hove
BN41 1WR

Published in Australia
Crabtree Publishing
Unit 3–5 Currumbin Court
Capalaba
QLD 4157

Contents

What are Grasslands? 4
Grasslands of the World 6
Canadian Prairies 8
American Prairies 10
Eurasian Steppe 12
Tibetan Plateau 14
South American Pampas 16
Llanos 18
African Savanna 20
Sahel 22
Veld 24
Australian Savanna 26
Grasslands in Danger 28
Glossary 30
Learning More 31
Index and About the Author 32

What are Grasslands?

A steaming **tropical rain forest**, a **parched desert** where the wind blows sand into huge **dunes**, a freezing Arctic **tundra** covered in snow and ice. These regions are very different from each other, but they have one thing in common—they are all **biomes**.

Amazing Biomes

A biome is an area that can be **classified** based on the types of plants and animals living there. The **climate**, soil type, and the amount of available water determine which plants and animals live there. For example, **taiga** is a biome that has long, cold winters and short, wet, mild summers. Most trees there are **conifers,** or evergreens, which keep their needles through the winter. The wolverines that live there have thick fur to help protect them from the cold. Other types of biomes include deserts, **wetlands**, and oceans.

A World of Grasslands

Grasslands are biomes that cover large parts of the planet. They are areas where the main plants are grasses, with only a few trees and shrubs. There are different reasons why trees cannot grow in grasslands. In some grasslands, it is too dry for trees to grow. In others, it is too cold, or it often floods.

Lions have sandy-colored coats that help them blend in with their surroundings.

Hunt or Be Hunted

A huge number of different animals live in the world's grasslands. Many of them are **grazers** and eat the grasses that grow there. Other animals hunt the grazers, often hiding in the tall grasses as they creep up on their **prey**.

GRASSLAND ANIMALS

MAP AND TRACK

The world's grasslands are home to a huge variety of animals, from enormous elephants to tiny insects. In this book, you will learn about many of these grassland animals. The "Map and Track" features will show you where grassland animals live. Build up your map-reading skills as you track their movements across the biome.

Zebras travel across the grasslands of Africa looking for fresh grass to eat.

*Black-necked cranes live in grasslands in Asia. These cranes are at risk of becoming endangered because their **habitat** is being destroyed.*

MORE GRASSLAND ANIMALS

STOP AND SPOT

As we travel around the world's grasslands, you will get a chance to take a close-up look at some of the **endangered** or threatened animals that live there in the "Stop and Spot" features throughout the book.

Grasslands of the World

Grasslands are all grassy—the clue is in the name! But apart from that, they can be very different. There are different kinds of grasslands found around the world: prairie, steppe, savanna, pampas, and veld are just a few of them.

This map shows all the grasslands that we will explore in this book.

Hot and Cold

Tropical grasslands are found near the **equator**. They have a warm climate. Savannas are a type of tropical grassland. The grasslands that are farther away from the equator are called **temperate** grasslands. They may still have hot summers, but they have cold winters, too, and are usually drier. Steppes are temperate grasslands.

Key

Temperate grasslands:

Canadian Prairies
American Prairies
Eurasian Steppe
Tibetan Plateau
South American Pampas

Tropical grasslands:

Llanos
African Savanna
Sahel
Veld
Australian Savanna

Where in the World?

There are grasslands on every continent except Antarctica. Grasslands are usually found between forests and deserts. Most grasslands receive less rain than forests, but more rain than most deserts. Most grasslands have deep, **fertile** soil. Many of them have been turned into farms, where farmers can grow crops such as wheat or corn.

Grassland Seasons

The climate in tropical grasslands is warm throughout the year, with a **dry season** and a **rainy season**. After the rains, they burst into life with beautiful wildflowers and grasses. Temperate grasslands usually get rain throughout the year, but only in small amounts. The grasses stop growing during the cold winters and begin again in spring.

Animals of the Grasslands

Grasslands support a huge variety of animal life. Their grasses are food for large grazing **mammals**, such as bison or antelope. These animals in turn become food for **predators** such as lions and coyotes. The long grasses and fertile soil provide homes for smaller animals. Birds build nests in the tall grasses, while prairie dogs dig holes and tunnels called **burrows** in the soil.

*The Eurasian Steppe can get very cold in the winter. Some animals **migrate** to warmer areas to find food.*

Canadian Prairies

Huge areas of Canada are covered with grassy prairies. These temperate grasslands take their name, "prairie," from the French word for "meadow." They were named by the French explorers who visited the area hundreds of years ago.

Red-tailed hawks save energy by soaring without flapping their wings.

North and South

The Canadian prairies are part of a larger grassland area that stretches south through the United States. They have hot summers and cold winters. The Canadian part of the prairie has colder temperatures, so many of its plants and animals are different from those farther south.

Prairie Animals

Large animals, such as deer and elk, graze on the grasses of the Canadian prairies. The grasslands are also home to a grazing animal called the pronghorn. Smaller animals, such as badgers, ground squirrels, and black-footed ferrets, hunt for food among the grasses. The flat land and short grasses make it easier for red-tailed hawks to spot prey from the sky. Small mammals, such as ground squirrels, hide from them in underground burrows.

As well as grasses, pronghorns eat the wildflowers and shrubs that grow on the prairies.

Changing Prairies

Most of the Canadian prairies have been turned into farmland. Less wild prairie land means less food for the animals that live there. Some **species**, including a bird called Sprague's pipit, have become threatened due to lack of food.

STOP AND SPOT

BLACK-FOOTED FERRETS

Black-footed ferrets live on the prairies, where they hunt prairie dogs. They sneak into burrows to catch sleeping prairie dogs. Disease, habitat loss, and farmers clearing land have reduced the number of prairie dogs, so the ferrets have less to eat. Now, black-footed ferrets are being bred in places such as zoos. They are then released into areas where there is enough food to support a growing number of ferrets.

Ferrets are not good diggers. They take over prairie dog burrows to raise their own young.

Prairie dogs live in groups and work together to watch out for predators such as hawks.

American Prairies

The prairies do not stop at the **border** with the United States. Instead, they extend south from Canada into warmer, drier areas. The American prairies are temperate grasslands. They are sometimes called the Great Plains. This region fills much of the area between the Mississippi River and the Rocky Mountains.

Tall and Short

In some areas of the American prairies, the grass grows very tall, with deep roots. In other areas, the grass is shorter. Grasses are tallest in the east, but they are shorter in the west, where there is less rain. These different prairie types are known as **tallgrass prairies** and **shortgrass prairies**. Between the two are **mixed-grass prairies**, which are a mix of the two types.

Helping the Soil

Prairie dogs are **rodents**, not dogs. They get their name from the barking sound they make. Prairie dog burrows can contain millions of animals! Their constant digging mixes up different types of soil, and the **nutrients** within it. This nutrient-rich soil helps healthier plants grow. This means better food for the animals that feed on the plants.

The prairie chicken is a type of grouse. It hides its nest in the thick grass.

Places to Hide

Many of the birds that live in the prairies are small and brown-colored, so they can blend in with the grasses. This helps to keep them and their nests safe from predators. In the flat grasslands, there are not many other places to hide.

BISON

Before European **settlers** arrived, plains bison grazed over huge areas of prairie in North America. The **Indigenous peoples** who lived there depended on bison for meat and animal skins. But in the 1800s, settlers began shooting bison in large numbers. By the 1880s, there were fewer than 1,000 bison left. Efforts were made to save the species, and now thousands of them live in **protected areas**.

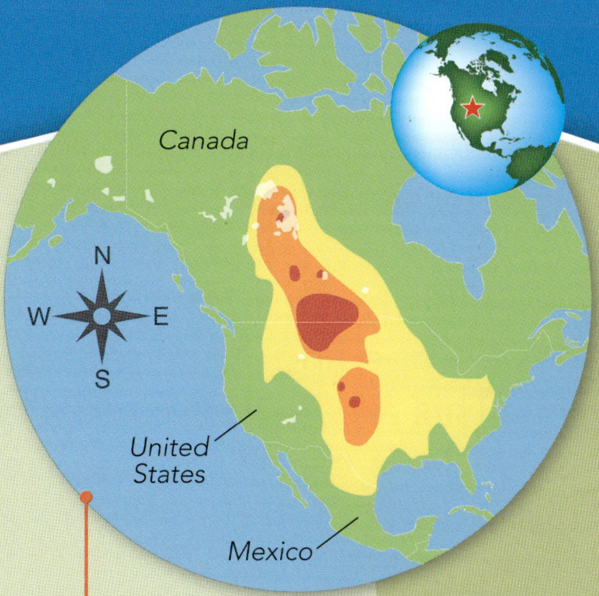

The yellow area shows where bison once lived. Their range shrank in the late 1800s.

Key
Original bison range
Bison range 1870
Bison range 1880
Current bison range

Many bison are raised on farms for their meat, but some still live wild on the prairies.

Eurasian Steppe

An absolutely enormous grassland stretches across Europe and Asia, from Hungary to eastern China. This area—the world's largest temperate grassland—is called the steppe. It is a vast sea of grass crisscrossed by rivers and streams.

Two Parts

The Altai Mountains divide the steppe into two sections: the western steppe and the eastern steppe. The eastern steppe is higher, colder, and drier. Both sections have cold winters and hot summers, but in the eastern half, the temperatures are even hotter or colder. Plants and animals living there must be tough to cope with the harsh conditions.

GREAT BUSTARDS

MAP AND TRACK

The great bustard is one of the world's largest flying birds. Males are up to 3 feet (1 m) tall, twice the size of females, and have neck hairs that look like long whiskers. Great bustards build their nests in the thick grasses of the steppes. During the winter, when the steppes are covered in snow, the bustards migrate to the south.

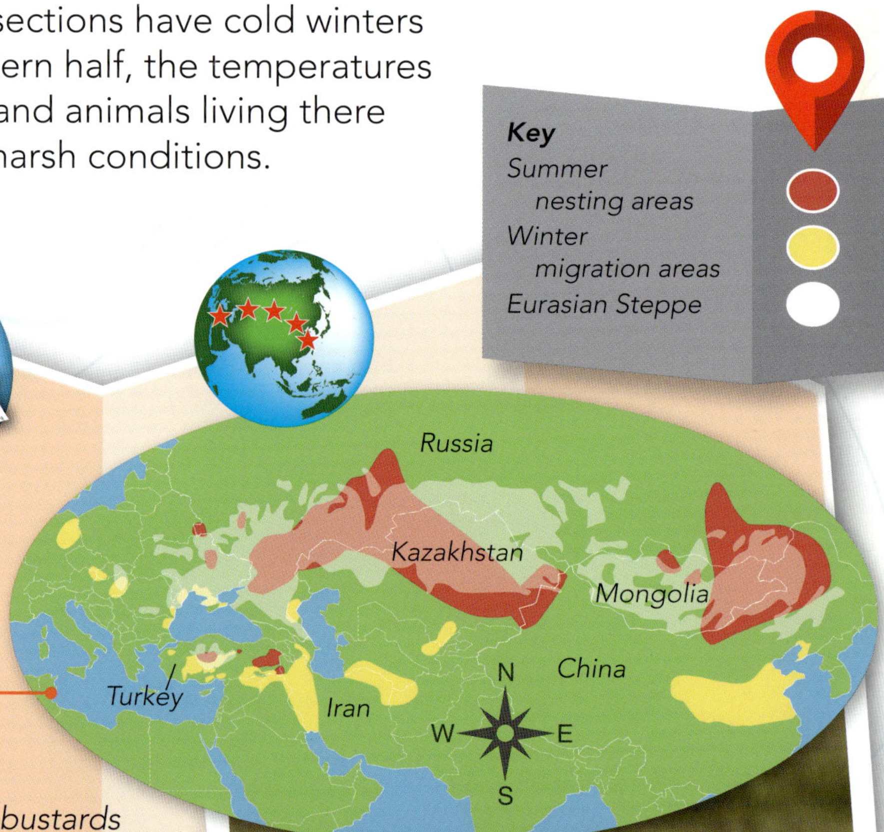

Great bustards gather in a few small areas during the winter.

A bustard's brown and cream feathers help it blend in with the steppe grasses.

Strange Snout

The saiga has a large humped snout that makes it one of the oddest-looking animals on the steppe. But this unusual nose is an **adaptation** to life on the steppe. In the summer, its snout helps **filter** out dust and cools the animal's blood. During the freezing winters, the snout warms the air before it reaches the animal's lungs, which helps keep the animal warm.

Herds of saigas graze on the steppe's grasses and drink from the rivers.

Steppe Animals

People have lived on the steppe for thousands of years, and they depended on horses to travel over the huge distances. A species of wild horse still lives on the steppe. Przewalski's horse grows longer fur during the cold winters.

Tibetan Plateau

Grasslands are everywhere—even on mountain **plateaus.** Trees cannot grow in the cold, windy, dry conditions, but grasses can. There are grasslands in many of the world's high places, including the vast Tibetan plateau in Asia. These grasslands are temperate.

Islands of Grass

Many mountain grasslands are fairly small areas, like islands of grass in a sea of a mountain landscape. Because they are cut off from other areas of the same type, the animals that live there are not often found anywhere else. The animals have adapted so they can live in these mountainous habitats.

Tibetan Plateau

The Tibetan plateau covers nearly 1 million square miles (2,590,000 sq km) in the region of southern China known as Tibet. It is sandwiched between some of the world's highest **mountain ranges.** Although the plateau itself is fairly flat, it is high above sea level. Large parts of the plateau are covered in grasslands.

The kiang's summer coat is short and sleek.

Animals of the Plateau

High in the mountains, the air has less of the **oxygen** that animals need to live. Animals there have adapted to cope with this, as well as with cold weather and dry conditions. For example, the plateau pika, a small mammal, has a high **heart rate**. This means its heart beats fast to keep oxygen pumping around its body. The kiang, a relative of the donkey, grows a thick coat of fur during winter to keep it warm.

STOP AND SPOT

ARGALIS

Argalis are large wild sheep that graze in mountain grasslands, including the Tibetan plateau. They are good climbers and often retreat to steep mountain slopes to escape from predators. Argalis live in groups called **herds**, which move across the plateau. They are now classified as endangered due to habitat loss. They also have to compete for grazing areas with large flocks of domestic sheep that are farmed for food.

Argalis pull up mouthfuls of young grass to eat.

*The burrows that pikas dig to keep warm and safe are often used by birds or small **reptiles** as shelters.*

South American Pampas

South America is famous for the Amazon rain forest, but the continent also has a huge area of temperate grassland in its southern half. This grassland, called the pampas, covers large parts of Argentina and Uruguay, and extends into southern Brazil.

Warm and Wet

The northern parts of the pampas are warmer and wetter, while the southern areas receive less than half as much rain. Grasses grow taller in the areas with more rain. The temperature in the southern parts still stays mild in the winter. Thunderstorms and strong winds, and even **tornadoes**, are common.

Pampas Animals

The rhea is a large flightless bird that looks a bit like an ostrich. When rheas run on their strong, long legs, they use their wings like **rudders** on a boat to change direction. This helps them run in a zigzag pattern to escape from predators such as pumas. Pumas are wild cats and are the largest predator in the region. Other pampas animals include guanacos, opossums, and rodents such as maras and cavies.

Rheas eat pampas plants as well as insects and other small animals.

Pampas Survivors

The pampas landscape is changing. Much of it is now used for farming and raising cattle, but many wild animals still live in the areas that remain untouched. Pampas deer graze on the region's grasses. Once there were many of these animals, but farming has made their habitat much smaller.

STOP AND SPOT

PAMPAS DEER

Pampas deer are fairly small, and when they sense danger, they often hide in the grasses before running a short distance away. One of the reasons they are at risk is that people hunt them. In Argentina, they are protected by law, but **poachers** still kill them for their meat and **hides**.

Only male pampas deer have antlers.

Guanacos live in herds and can run fast to escape predators.

Llanos

The northern part of South America is home to another large grassland. The Llanos covers parts of Venezuela and Colombia. Unlike the pampas, the Llanos is a tropical grassland. It is warm and wet all year round.

Scarlet ibis chicks are gray and brown. They soon turn red because of the red shellfish that they eat.

Rivers and Grass

The mighty Orinoco River flows through the Llanos, and there are several smaller rivers as well. This means the Llanos gets more water than most other tropical grasslands. Parts of the Llanos flood during the rainy season, turning it into a wetland. Because of the flooding, most of the land is not suitable for growing crops, but many ranchers let their cattle graze there.

The Llanos are home to capybaras, the world's largest rodent. An adult capybara can be the size of a big dog.

Bursting with Life

There is a huge range of animal life in the Llanos. The rivers and wetlands are home to caimans and crocodiles, as well as turtles, such as the Arrau sideneck turtle. There are also many types of wading birds, including the scarlet ibis, which gathers in large flocks.

Mammals of the Llanos

Capybaras gather in groups on riverbanks and lakeshores to feed on grasses and water plants. Their eyes and nostrils are on the tops of their heads, so they can hide in the water. They are a favorite meal of the jaguars that live in the Llanos. These large cats also hunt many other animals, including deer and tapirs.

MAP AND TRACK

GIANT ANTEATERS

Giant anteaters sniff out termite or ant nests, and tear them open with their sharp claws. They use their long, sticky tongues to collect the insects. Apart from mothers with babies, most giant anteaters live alone. Each giant anteater has a **home range** where it lives and looks for food.

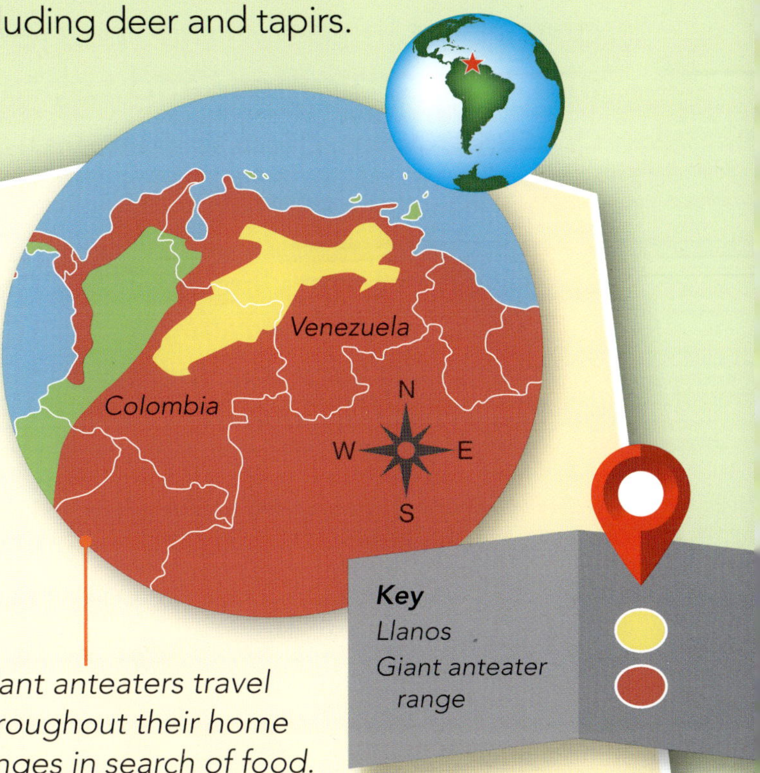

Giant anteaters travel throughout their home ranges in search of food.

Giant anteaters live across large parts of South America, including the Llanos.

African Savanna

The savanna in Africa may be the most famous grassland in the world. Large animals, such as elephants, giraffes, and zebras, roam this tropical grassland. Lions and other predators hunt them.

Savanna Landscape

The savanna covers large parts of Africa. These regions separate the rain forest in the center of the continent from the drier areas to the north and south. Unlike many other grasslands, this savanna has quite a few trees. It is warm all year round. It stays dry for most of the year, but there is a rainy season in the summer months.

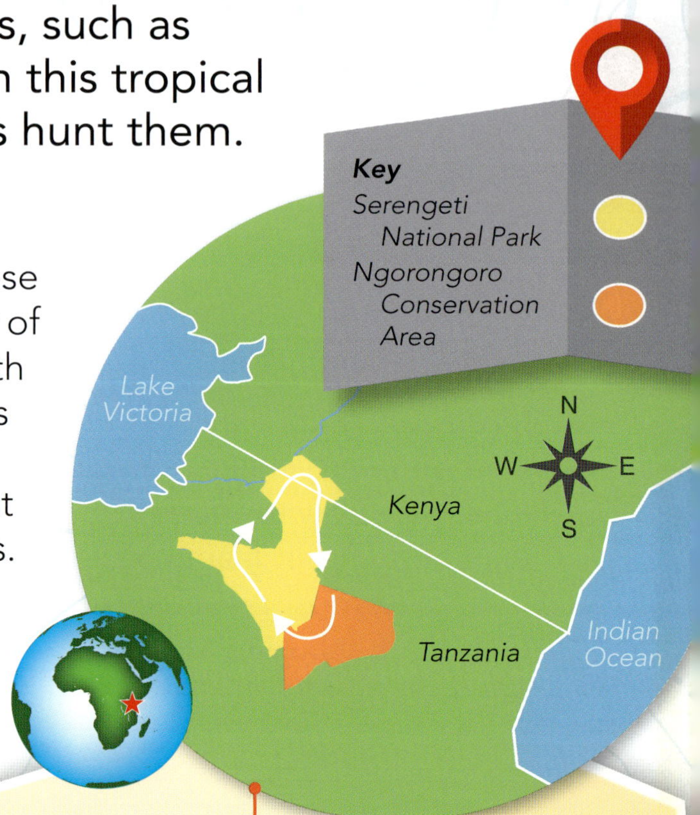

Wildebeests begin moving north in April, then head south in November. Their route takes them through conservation areas.

MAP AND TRACK

WILDEBEESTS

Wildebeests are large antelopes that graze on the savanna. They travel in large herds through Kenya and Tanzania. Wildebeests follow the rains as they look for fresh, green grass that the rains bring. Every year, millions of them migrate along a route that is like a large loop. This route takes them across several large rivers, where crocodiles lie in wait.

Wildebeest calves must learn to run as soon as they are born to escape from lions and other predators.

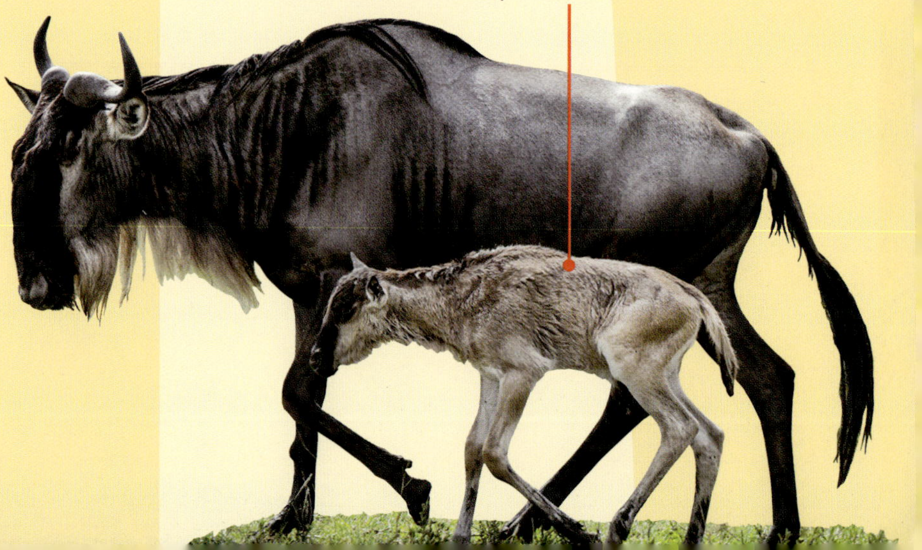

Grazers, Big and Small

Huge numbers of animals gather to graze on the savanna. Smaller animals, such as antelopes, eat grasses. Giraffes use their long necks to reach up into acacia trees. Their long tongues pull off the leaves while avoiding the acacia's sharp thorns. But the trees release chemicals that make their leaves taste bitter, so the animals do not destroy the tree completely.

Savanna Predators

All these grazers mean that there is plenty of food for the predators who live on the savanna. **Prides**, or groups, of lions work together to hunt large prey, including giraffes and buffalo. Cheetahs use their speed to chase down faster prey, such as gazelles. Secretary birds hunt smaller prey, such as insects and snakes. Vultures and hyenas **scavenge** their meals from the kills of larger predators.

Elephants and zebras are just two of the grazing species that depend on the savanna's grasses.

Sahel

The savanna is not Africa's only tropical grassland. A drier region called the Sahel stretches from east to west across the continent. The Sahel is an area where the land changes from the dry Sahara Desert in the north to the wetter savanna in the south. Its name, Sahel, is from the **Arabic** word for "coast."

Dry Grassland

The Sahel is much drier than the savanna, and there are fewer trees. Large parts of the region receive less than 10 inches (25 cm) of rain a year during a short rainy season. Over the last 70 years or so, farming and **drought** have affected the Sahel. Parts of it have lost their grasses and soil, and have turned into **barren** wastelands.

Grazers of the Sahel

There used to be large populations of grazers in the Sahel. But farmers have brought in herds of **livestock**, forcing many of the wild animals into protected areas. Herds of gazelles still survive in these areas, where they are hunted by lions and cheetahs. Dorcas gazelles jump into the air when they spot a predator. This behavior is called "stotting." It shows the predator how fit the gazelle is, and it alerts other gazelles to the danger.

Male dorcas gazelles use their horns to fight off other males. They survive in the dry Sahel because they get all the water they need from their food.

STOP AND SPOT

AFRICAN WILD DOGS

The African wild dog lives in areas across Africa. They hunt in packs to bring down prey. The wild dog is endangered due to habitat loss, catching diseases from domestic dogs, and being hunted by other predators, such as lions.

The patterns on each dog's coat are different.

Sahel Monkeys

Several species of **primates** have adapted to live in the dry, mostly treeless landscape of the Sahel. Unlike many other monkeys, the patas monkey lives close to the ground. There are not many hiding places in the Sahel, but patas monkeys are fast runners, so they can escape from predators that way.

Patas monkeys search for insects, seeds, and roots to eat.

Veld

In southern Africa, there is a type of grassland called the veld. Its open plains are covered with grasses and shrubs. Veld covers large parts of South Africa, Botswana, Namibia, and Zimbabwe. "Veld" comes from the **Afrikaans** word for "field." The veld is a tropical grassland.

Hot and Dry

Some areas of the veld are less than 2,000 feet (610 m) above sea level. These are called the lowveld. Other areas rise to 6,000 feet (1,829 m) or more, with steep-sided hills called kopjes. Most of the rainfall in the veld comes from thunderstorms during the summer months. Winters are mild, and droughts are common.

MAP AND TRACK

SOUTHERN AFRICAN ROCK PYTHONS

The Southern African rock python is one of the largest snakes on the continent. It is long and heavy, and it kills prey by squeezing it to death. It then stretches its jaws wide to swallow the animal whole. These huge snakes need water and survive the veld's long dry season by becoming **dormant**.

The rock python lives throughout the southern part of the continent.

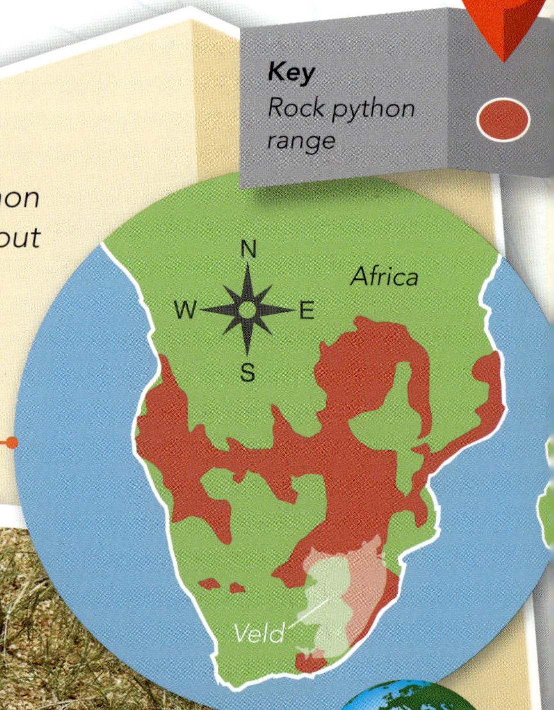

The patterns on its scales help the rock python blend in with its surroundings.

Dung beetles feed on the feces, or waste, of larger animals, often rolling it into balls.

The "Big Five"

Visitors come to the veld hoping to see all the "big five" African animals: lions, elephants, buffalo, leopards, and rhinoceroses. But the area is home to huge numbers of other animals, including bats, birds, snakes, and porcupines. Grazing mammals often travel in large mixed herds for safety. Zebras have good eyesight for seeing predators across the veld, while wildebeests have better hearing. When these animals graze together, they are more likely to keep safe.

Protecting Veld Wildlife

Large parts of the veld are now used for farming and ranching, forcing out many of the wild animals. In addition, people have hunted the veld's large animals for sport. All of this has negatively affected the wildlife. For example, there are now only a few thousand south-central black rhinoceroses left. However, large areas of the veld are now set aside as wildlife **reserves**, which are places where animals are kept safe. Most of the veld's larger animals, such as elephants and leopards, mainly live in these reserves.

Australian Savanna

A large area of tropical grassland stretches across northern Australia, covering nearly one-quarter of the continent. These dry areas have few trees, but in deep **gullies**, there are areas of rain forest.

Wildfires

Fierce fires often sweep across Australia's tropical savanna. Most of them are started by people. During the short wet season, grasses grow tall, then dry out when the rains stop. In these conditions, even small fires can quickly get out of control. Luckily, many savanna plants are adapted to survive fire. Under the ground, the roots of the grasses are not damaged. After the fire, new shoots grow back from the roots. Some animals can survive fires by hiding in holes and burrows.

MAP AND TRACK

CANE TOADS

In the 1930s, a species of beetle was destroying Australia's sugarcane crops. To try to control the beetles, about 100 cane toads from Hawaii were released into the crop areas, with the hopes that they would eat the beetles. However, the cane toad population grew rapidly and spread beyond the crop areas. Cane toads eat other wildlife, not just sugarcane beetles, which means there is less prey for other species. Larger animals die after eating the poisonous cane toads.

The map shows the range of the cane toad in Australia.

*Cane toads are an **invasive** species that cause serious problems in Australia.*

Savanna Animals

The savanna is home to a wide variety of animals. Wallabies and kangaroos graze on grasses, while bats called flying foxes feed on **nectar** and fruit. There is a huge range of birds, from enormous emus that cannot fly to tiny finches. Large lizards, such as goannas, hunt other animals.

Terrific Termites

Towering termite mounds are a familiar sight on the savanna. The tiny insects that build these nests play an important role in keeping the biome healthy. They take in nutrients from eating dead wood and grass. Some of these nutrients go into the mounds, and when the mounds **decompose**, or rot, and break down, the nutrients go back into the soil. Other animals take in nutrients when they eat the termites.

Large termite mounds can be 26 feet (8 m) tall.

Grasslands in Danger

Many of the world's grasslands are in danger. Farming, building homes, and **climate change** have all helped to reduce and destroy grasslands. Many **conservation groups** are working to protect grasslands and the plants and animals that live there.

A flock of sheep eats a lot of grass. The sheep may not leave enough for the wild animals to eat.

Wildlife Reserves

Over the past centuries, huge areas of prairie, savanna, and steppe have been turned into farmland. This has meant the loss of lots of the plants and animals that live there. Grasses are replaced with crops. Livestock such as cattle and sheep push out **native species**. Setting some areas aside as wildlife reserves can help animals survive.

The black rhinoceros is one of many endangered grassland animals.

Climate Change

Earth's average temperature is slowly rising, and weather patterns are changing. Some areas now have more rain than before, and some have less. Droughts, fires, and storms may become more common. Grassland plants and animals will have to adapt to the new conditions if they are to survive.

MAP AND TRACK IT!

Now it is your turn. You can create a map to track endangered grassland animals. Here is what you need to do:

1. Choose one of the grasslands in this book.
2. Create a map to show the grassland (see page 6 for help).
3. Research the animals that live in the grassland you have chosen. Which ones are endangered? Choose two or three endangered animals to track.
4. Color in the map to show where they are found. See the box below to learn how to find map references for your chosen animals.
5. Make a key to show what the different colors mean.

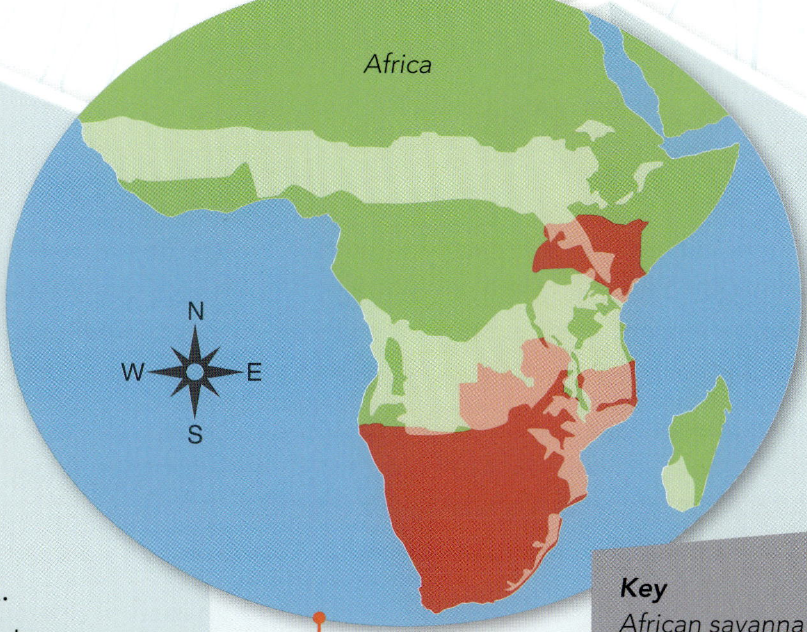

Key
African savanna
White rhinoceros range

If you chose to map and track the white rhinoceros, your map would look like this.

THE IUCN

The International Union for Conservation of Nature (IUCN) is a great place to look for your map. The IUCN is an international group of scientists that track animals and decide whether they are endangered. They produce reports on many different species, including maps to show where they currently live. The website for their "Red List," where you can search by species, is on page 31.

Glossary

Please note: Some **bold-faced** words are defined where they appear in the text.

adaptation Changing over time to be better able to live in a certain environment

Afrikaans Language based on the Dutch that is spoken in South Africa

Arabic A language spoken widely across the Middle East and northern Africa

barren Unable to support life

biomes Large geographical areas with the same general landscape, climate, and life

border An imaginary line that forms the boundary between two countries or regions

burrows Holes or tunnels dug by an animal to use as a hiding place or a home

classified Arranged in a certain order

climate Weather conditions in a region

climate change A change in weather patterns due to Earth's temperature getting warmer

conservation groups Organizations that work to protect nature

desert A biome that gets very little rain and often has very few plants

dormant In a resting state that saves energy when an animal eats little food

drought A long period of time with less than the normal amount of rainfall

dry season A period of the year in tropical areas when very little rain falls

endangered At risk of dying out

equator An imaginary line around the middle of Earth

fertile Able to produce lots of crops

filter To pass through something to remove unwanted material

gullies Small valleys or trenches carved out by running water

habitat The natural environment of an animal or plant

hides Animal skins used for clothing

Indigenous peoples Original inhabitants of a region or country, sometimes called First Nations, Aboriginal, or Native people

invasive Spreading and causing harm

livestock Animals that are not wild and are raised or kept on a farm or ranch instead

mammals Warm-blooded animals that have hair and produce milk to feed their young

migrate To move from one place to another, often traveling to the same location each year

mountain ranges Series of mountains arranged in a line and connected by high ground

native species Animals normally found in a certain habitat

nectar A sugary fluid made by a flower

oxygen A gas in the air that all living things need to breathe to stay alive

parched Having very little moisture

plateaus Large areas of high, flat land

poachers People who hunt illegally

predators Animals that kill and eat other animals

prey Animals that are killed and eaten by another animal for food

primates A group of mammal species that includes monkeys, apes, and humans

protected areas Land set aside just for animals to keep them safe

rain forest Tropical forests that have a lot of rain and very tall trees

rainy season A period of the year in tropical areas when huge amounts of rain fall

reptiles Cold-blooded animals such as snakes, lizards, and turtles

rodents Mammals with long front teeth that never stop growing

scavenge To eat food that has been left behind by others

settlers People who come to a new area to make their homes

species A distinct type of living thing

temperate Having a temperature that is not too hot and not too cold

tornadoes Storms with very high winds that spin in a funnel shape

tropical Having a hot and wet climate

tundra A flat, treeless Arctic biome

wetlands Areas of land, such as marshes or swamps, often covered with shallow water

Learning More

Books

Bernhardt, Carolyn. *Super Simple Grassland Projects: Fun & Easy Animal Environment Activities* (Awesome Super Simple Habitat Projects). Super Sandcastle, 2016.

Bow, James. *Grasslands Inside Out* (Ecosystems Inside Out). Crabtree Publishing Company, 2014.

Callery, Sean. *Life Cycles: Grassland*. Kingfisher, 2018.

Spilsbury, Louise, and Richard Spilsbury. *Grassland Biomes* (Earth's Natural Biomes). Crabtree Publishing Company, 2018.

Websites

www.iucnredlist.org/search
Explore the IUCN's Red List of animals that are threatened, endangered, or nearly extinct.

http://kids.nceas.ucsb.edu/biomes/grassland.html
Find out more about North American grasslands and the animals that live there.

www.nationalgeographic.org/media/african-savanna-illustration
Learn more about the grasslands in Africa and the animals that live there.

svs.gsfc.nasa.gov/2285
Discover NASA's satellite data showing an animated globe of the world's grasslands.

Index

adaptations 13, 14, 23, 26, 28
African savanna 6, 20–21
American prairies 6, 10–11
Antarctica 6
anteaters 19
antelopes 7, 13, 19, 20, 21
argalis 15
Australian savanna 6–7, 20–21
big cats 4, 7, 16, 19, 20, 21, 22, 23, 25
biomes 4, 5, 27
birds 5, 7, 8, 9, 10, 12, 15, 16, 18, 21, 25, 27
bison 7, 11
black-footed ferrets 8, 9
blending in with surroundings 4, 10, 12, 24
Canadian prairies 6, 8–9
cane toads 26
capybaras 18
climate change 28
crocodiles 18, 20
deer 8, 16, 17, 19
droughts 22, 24, 28
elephants 20, 21, 25
endangered animals 5, 15, 23, 28, 29
Eurasian Steppe 6–7, 12–13, 28
farming 6, 9, 11, 15, 16, 22, 25, 28
flooding 4, 18
gazelles 21, 22
giraffes 20, 21
grazing animals 4, 7, 8, 11, 13, 15, 16, 18, 20, 21, 22, 25, 27
great bustards 12
habitat loss 5, 9, 15, 16, 23, 26
Indigenous peoples 11
insects 16, 19, 21, 23, 25, 27
lions 4, 7, 20, 21, 22, 23
Llanos 6, 18–19
mammals 7, 8, 19, 25
mountain grasslands 6, 12, 14–15
native species 28
patas monkeys 23
pikas 14, 15
prairie dogs 7, 9, 10
prairies 6, 8–9, 10–11
predators 4, 7, 9, 10, 15, 16, 17, 20, 21, 23, 25
protected areas 11, 17, 22
Przewalski's horse 13
rain forests 4, 16, 20, 26
rainfall 6, 7, 10, 16, 18, 20, 22, 24, 26, 28
rhinoceroses 25, 28, 29
Sahel 6, 22–23
saigas 13
savannas 6, 20, 21, 22, 26, 27, 28
scavengers 21
snakes 21, 24, 25
South American pampas 6, 16–17, 18
temperate grasslands 6–7, 8–9, 10–11, 12–13, 14–15, 28
termites 27
Tibetan plateau 6–7, 14–15
trees 4, 14, 20, 21, 22, 23, 26
tropical grasslands 6–7, 18–19, 20–21, 22–23, 24–25, 20–21
veld 6, 24–25
wetlands 4, 18
wild dogs 23
wildebeests 20
wildlife reserves 25, 28
zebras 5, 20, 21, 25

ABOUT THE AUTHOR

Nancy Dickmann has written more than 130 nonfiction books for children, specializing in science. Before becoming an author, she worked for many years as an editor and publisher of children's books. She has traveled through many different grasslands, including the African savanna, where she was able to see her favorite grassland animal, the giraffe, in the wild.